C000132314

Princess Daniela, enjoying her free time away from the pipe. epic Le Diablerets

freedom

While hiking a late March wind drift - this X-Games Champion and overall Swiss Euro chick guru - Daniela Roth - asks me what I really thought of freestyle snowboard competition? With an off hand shrug, I convey that I had mixed feelings on the subject...

She seemed some-what surprised by my abstract response, which in turn surprised me. I mean, does anyone seriously agree with the words 'freestyle' and 'competition' being used in the same phrase - it's an oxymoron. Yet I'm sure Daniela, along with other cutting edge riders out there, take great pride in their quest for balance recognition. But are they free?

Freestyle in my belief is a contradiction to competition because it simply means life at your own level, no outside rules except respect for others, in being free and looking for style - love and epic feeling cherished true. Through every moment, during every day.

Competition, on the other hand, is about following guidelines so you may be judged equally against another. Which isn't always easy and in the end just boils down to an industry examination test, another school report, queue for the glory trade. And quite frankly, the spectators couldn't care less. When it comes to balance enjoyment, people just wanna see us ride and dance the sky, push those limits and release some cry, maybe someday have a try. That's why real jam-style events are the only ones that make it to truly epic status - because we see the truth through easy corruptionless design. Skip the fine-print bullshit and the hard way - just get together and party!

Take the development of any free-competition scene for example, there are always dilemmas encountered with trying to put these people into a box, because freedom & love are limitless! Evolutionary thanks to the surfer for lessons in this. Do you know the feeling? Do you know what exactly constitutes freedom? Please write in and share your wisdom...

Obviously, there are many racial, social, and mental minorities that understand exactly what freedom might mean - if they had it. So we must consider people whose ancestry hasn't conformed with the wealth that usually accompanies real freedom. The ones who missed out on early balance encouragement and had to jump their nest in search of inner energy to spend on dreams. Riders who may never have the circumstance to make this high new century grade of sponsored competition, yet are still equally free. This storybook and the ones to follow, are written for the people, the brotherhood - simple ideas toward freedom and better living.

I guess you can say it's all just about keeping beat with an oblivious drummer, while treating any rare moment of heavenly perfection to simply ride and not focus on any sub standard judgements or the many uncomfortable details there-in. Quietly searching for higher balance in what we try and thus wider freedom in any life we choose. Me and you.

To make things easier I figured it best to dig out a couple of facts, history and things from our world, then 180 shovit them inside a big freedom bonanzza storybook. So you can use your own given rights to think and act for yourself. Read, practice and compare. Rid despair. And feel welcomed to the complete life of freeriding. True freeriding - no competition. For sure a little rebellion and laughter, maybe a wise crack or two, but nothing at all serious. Just some smooth rhymes for our friends to escape with and happily break those shackles, remembering life is a personal choice.

Skate, snow, surf, sky
real life no cry
warm winter
smooth reading
global premier
wise to healing
mountain bike two
whole life thru
les storybook
power for truth!

sketch by nuey

welcome to our epic storybook

Concept inspired by the lives of nuey, waza, slug, mousta, eagle, ol'yella, big bird, m-bro, dirty dave, gumby, pit bull, sooky, zam, TD, dabu, shmoo, gibbo, mitch, mero, mario, mum, one eye, shanky, beep beep, the g's, jules, jah & serendipity soul..

produced with-in the law of summit heartcore inquiries through website www.epicbalance.com via facebook or on a chair next epic powder day!

storyteller
epicscope
creative
intelligence

guest photography ©
christophe margot
pat vermeulen
jason childs
trav garone
alan long
tim lewis
cyril neri
justin field
epic friends
shirley costa
mike truelove
cruzy suzzette
alice in wonderland

peter corney
no fixed address
contact me on FB or
epicscope.com.au

© art by
nick mcnally,
andy shuttleworth,
richard brownfield,
spun bros, urchin &
nicolas vaudroz

additional words from fabio, slug, tomba, gibbo, nuey & ron

design & photo assistance
justin field & nick mcnally

COVER the silhouette of a freeskier, craig moegel at home in falls creek - photography by pea ce.

poetry for the people originally published in 2002 then proudly re-released in 2012 & 2020 © Epicscope.

ISBN 978-0-9581930-0-9

Other than standard referencing for media review, copy reproduction or distribution in any way, shape or by any means, requires respectful approval from the storyteller.

Proudly an epic profit-share production.

Seriously, names don't mean shit, actions are what count, people in action - noble mouth. So come on people, stand up for your rights. Choose to get freedom and say goodbye to boredom. Always respect others, even through the pain, then all will respect you, for being true again and again. Pat ya mate on the back, it sure gives good medicine, but diss the inconvenience of glorification. This is a read about living, not ass lick'n. Kick back and relax, there's no rush in our kitchen. Deepest appreciation to all who help out, mostly to the ones who need no thanks (your share is the greatest). Plus all our friends who say this will work, nothing can thank you enough for such gifts. If we truly believe we will definitely achieve. Chicata

poetry for the people

alan long photo

enter own risk

WHY - under or over - white lies - horseshoe groove - costatom
see life sideways - gibbo's crack at the jackpot - O' how free
artists at work + some other stoke to get you fired up!

It was the freerider that brought us home. The freedom fighter who lives life to the bone. Boarders bred from surf, plankers hot on the buzz, city rats pure on skate, on balance, showing us the way - many thanks! We knew we wanted to be like you, yet often sold on negativity blue. Visions of heaven, witness to struggle, fighting for rights with courage to burst bubbles. Simple question corruptionist blind. Proud and tall for our choice to ride. One day beyond survive. Mmmm, it was the freerider that brought us home. Once the brat, confused, false judgement clone. Learning lessons to remember the tribesman stone. And even though technology change, our feeling of vibrations remain the same. Love to you, salute the crew, Andy Mero going huge! Remember the day, live it now. The nobles who ride are very proud.

The original SBR big air - justin

10

under or over?

nobody really knows. Except of course yourself. Please feel free and comment.

28

horseshoe groove...

photo poetry
nomad blue
hometown
spirits,
local truth
global
characters
forever rule.

54

costa tom

He's not just the greatest skier on the planet, some times he's the worst. Just an ordinary bloke standing up against slavery.

I'm not
sure when it
started, just that
it was dumping out the
window when I awoke, and it
didn't stop for days. Until it felt like it
always was and always would be there.

First session, boot to knee. second,
funnelling up my waist. third, no need
to turn except to escape the slides. on
the forth day I was wishing I had powder
boards. AK Launchers or those Dynastar
fatty's - 190, no 200, or bigger! It was so
ridiculously deep we couldn't believe it!
I even started getting blasé about it. Yet,
as soon as it looked like leaving, wind
crusting or getting all tracked, we found
our selves madly hiking for more. hunting
it, wondering where it was hiding, when
it would come next and why it had to
disappear so soon.

That's the life, the buzz of the hunt,
the adrenaline in the ride, the lifestyle.
Freestyle, freesoul, freeride - everything
else is just how you get there. The grind
and exhilaration of travel. Scraping up the
change for an air ticket, some new boots,
or fresh sticks when an edge blows out or
your bindings tweak when you land airs.

Mountains are the mission. Working in
smoky bars 'til four in the morning, so
you can get first chair at nine. Listening
to roots, reggae and funk music,
keeping it all rolling from season to
season. The physic, the finance, the
inspiration to improve your riding, your
life, the honour of great friendships and
the stoke of every new day in the alpine.
A million lines to ride, one life to live.

craig moegel

Damien "Schmoo" Roberts grinding the 'zza for some life - justin

peter 'pea ce' corney by christophe margot

WHY will everybody finally get it? We are freeriders -nothing more & nothing less. That's what I am about & what I have always dreamed of being. The maintenance engineering, pizza pete, the hospitality, snowmaking, MC, photography, the business & design, even these words - are tools I acquire to ride more. Just things to fill the gaps until I am practicing balance again. Achieving it. Healing myself & helping others who want it too. And at times I have found unbalance, feeling like it's a world gone wrong. Redemption song. Yet it is still a world of my own creation, so I look for balance in everything I dream. Practicing on a trampoline. To touch the mountain, walk a wave, ride my skate - pure balanced state. To stoke out on another's smile, for it is a smile quite of my style. Then while at this place where everything is epic -at one with nature, in awe of how perfect, simply connected, communicating beyond words - I give respect to everybody & present to you our storybook. May the people rejoice!

Under or Over?

A few people poorly remarked that the **Summit Board Riders** had faded, died, to a certain extent relinquished their rights to serve.

Yet, like all shit talk, this is not our truth. Those who feel the mountain close & real laugh aloud. Blasphemy comes from the fearful who turn their backs, spit into the wind & live on the dark side.

We feel it deep in our hearts that epic freeriders live on, no less than yesterday, never as good as tomorrow. Gold & royalty. Trees & perfect alpine pitch. Friendship. Honest, look-ya-mate-in-the-eye friendship. Respect. Through the ups & downs heartcore people always commit to freedom from prejudice & promotion of balance in all its forms.

This is the hallmark of our evolution in free space. If everyone thinks their burden is the heaviest, then those on a quest for epic balance are no different. Sleeping in subways, doing those dashes for transport - trains, planes & smokey vans, to escape the worlds of fear. To find the source of love. Scored when we've been good. Shamed if mistaken. Always on the same track headed for higher truth. To create epic worlds for you, because we are one.

Anybody can present themselves as different but on the inside we are all alike. Lets treat everyone the same, help each other stay out of the rain. Life toward balance, less & less pain. If we are to take drugs for any dis-ease, which ones are best please? How much true to take? What rate? When to stop? Why are some hidden with no facts or help? Yet people abuse them & deny this causes hell. How about no drugs at all - fly high stand tall. We are epic stories about life. Trusting to catch the right flight. Finding it in our hearts to give generously to the plight. Creating movie light.

It's funny if you're a suck - you will. If you're a god - you'll shine. See those who seek reference to a better time. Will they return? Where have they been? Is it just an alcoholic dream? There are some who'd shadow people they don't know, yet silence in their eyes - coward act little respect. How come we aren't all perfect? Big head not free. There has to be balance through to the feet. Do you contribute or do you scorn? Misunderstanding is the back-stabber's lawn. Ordinary people, yet awake. Complete the education & make up for mistakes.

dirty dave & ronnie dabu © Epic.

pea ce © juzzie whistler sojourn circa 1994

pea ce © nuey headwater halfpipe falls creek circa 2001

13

Under or Over?

Help us recognise each and every flaw. Talk openly please, lay witness to universal law. Easy laugh at sleep talking negativity - reference gifts escaping obscurity. Everything we see, is it a mirror of me? Individual worlds, here to help all smile. Don't stand shy, jump the epic mile. Families with hearts, children true, support a brotherhood that is made up of you. Recognise the physical is third part whole. Question the questions, why dig holes? Have faith in answers, recognition strong - that freeriders have an everlasting bond.

Balance the voice, freedom soul. Mother earth happy knowing we'll all live on. Spirit of life, nobility & cool. Balanced community, no more hating school. More & more royalty, acting with dignity, freedom of choice, sharing the wealth in our dynasty. People of the forest, life to the core, more & more beauty - happy to be raw. Reduce the struggle discomfort a bore. If you separate any life the family will re-store. Until we all discover our togetherness need. If we are just one, why should another bleed? It's important to state that the burdens we face, are not designed to last. Just to be remembered as we realise our true force.

Heaven is actually right here on earth. Everyone has their own hands and unique choice. Quit with just love only for the cream, our mothers milk is better complete. Respect silence in belief & understand there is relief. The highest truth, thanks for the pain - without it we would have never discovered the same. All eyes who choose this search so close - face the challenge & go balance berserk! Pride in the ride, steady growth. Any form strong, till you score an epic horn. Healthy herbs, women are free. Life from the heart - core you and me.

Freeride infinitive, dream dedication, pushing the limits across all nations. Support your heros, help their dreams be true. Come together as partners, immaculate scream in two. With heart felt motive, together media trust, inspiration everywhere cause we're on the same bus. Event standardisation, pro realization. Music groove culture, holistic sensation. Health a fact - wild animals are prancing. Everyone totally happy with a life full of dancing. Own realisations true, we march as warriors to help others come through. Many thanks for those who already knew..

pipe eagle pea ce by nuey

Studying the fundamental logistics of developing holistic balance stadiums, our warrior measures the minimum dome height for a GTR halfpipe complex.

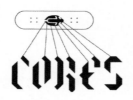

In design the best work
always comes from the heart.
Same is true throughout life,
whether it's a snowpark or a surf break
with freedom to harmonise for people,balance
& stoke, or the spirit behind epic balance parks
in urban culture - we are everywhere, singing
the story of friends who roam wild. On mountains
& down the coast. Across concrete. In the air.
We are true, sharing ideas toward liberation & freedom.
Not unlike you. Wepride on involvement only if actions
benefit everything they affect. No compromise. Simply
here to laugh at the corruptionists until they can
laugh at themselves. It's only the fear.
We are part of the cure. It's possible
one of us is already one of you.

Introducing
the summit heartcore
Freeride infinitive

experience

fresh air

new world

consulting

Born as a boardriding group during the last millenia end.
Evolving true heart presence as we overcome discrimination
and miseducation - through multi-world travels, epic adventures
and a constant effort for higher balance. We are part of the growing
consciousness that everything is one! All of it, everywhere - connected.

A very successful perspective.
Feel free and share your story...

music from the box - various - sounds of spirit...

Charlies snow angels

THE ANDREW SHUTTLEWORTH EXPERIENCE

Slightly
exaggerated,
warped to a degree,
proportionally sarcastic,
these pictures
drawn to please.
Marginally twisted,
with a hint of obscurity
but if you look hard enough
there are truths aplenty
something about love
and freedom
mentality.

Twisted chick

Bricks and steel

Hard days night

Bearly

Contemplation

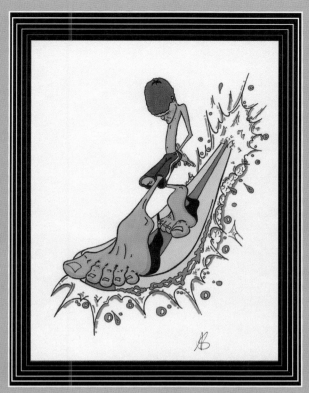

Toes of soul

Woody

Mans best friend

horseshoe GROOVE

The funniest thing about trying to describe the local scene at Horseshoe Creek is that there isn't one. Hang on, I'll take that back. There is and there isn't. A local is generally someone with concrete ties or background related to a specific location. The only confusion with H.C. is that the majority of it's inhabitants are blow-ins from some where else - which leaves this renamed paradise with little, if any, historic flavour. Thus, few locals.

Walking along Slalom Street it's hard to spot a classic mountain goat, someone who really looks like they've been hanging here their whole life. If such people exist then they're hiding out beside log fires, devoting hospitality for exclusive guests. Horseshoe Creek is yet to boast cobble stone streets, designer stores or alpine institutes, but where she lacks economic roots, this lady booms with some of the sweetest freeriding in Oz. Including terrain parks the Summit Boardriders developed, that got so good it was a hard kept secret. Throw in the Summit Bowl, Rock Garden and a myriad of lines that grace International Poma. Making love carves down the Y's or taking a hike over to Mount Mackay (steep south face lines and front side windies). What about six minutes in a helicopter to hustle at Mt H? It's easy to see why more of us are calling ourselves Heartcore.

H.C. and Mt H, if joined by commerce, seem so big that one all encompassing scene is out of the question. The commanding villages may well be quaint enough to accommodate such unity, but vast cultural diversity of it's inhabitants, along with their wilbury circumstance, have made it more like several distinct sub-scenes. Dispersed throughout the areas gallery of bowls, hits, trees and back country, there's one thing for sure - you'll hear whispers of legendary characters jamming that infamous park over at Horseshoe. or generations of friends hanging within amber sniff of the Bird over on Mt H.

Hotham intimidates the punters. It appears to be a wind blown, ultra-challenging outpost for the hearty rich, but it's true beauty lies somewhere amongst wilderness around the area boundary. Secret little stashes that only local rats know and go to. Underground characters who live for laughter down special runs - holding onto sensory overload, turn after turn.

Fly back creek side, with all the family types out making nice easy turns on the wide groomed runs, and you'll stumble upon a jibbers dream. An easily digestible maze of trees, hits, powder and rock outcrops. The kind of labyrinth only those who put in the time have figured out. The magic of Horseshoe is what keeps regulars coming back. None of the gully steeps of it's windy neighbour, or huge fall line of Thredas, but a mix and match of an old coastal roadie, which keeps everyone amused.

There's no debate about how epic the Summit and International are when fresh snow hits town. Plus the biking around these parts in summer is nothing short of all-time. I've seen bros find and drop hidden lines that I'm sure very few know are there, let alone the mind, heart and courage to score. On any powder day, the feeling lift-side is powerful with everyone buzzing adrenalin from their last turns. If the lift line is long, try sneaking in behind one of the snow sport instructors. Falls' has one of the largest snow sport schools in Australia - so it should be easy. Some of those hodads are the strongest talent in town too. Bust through the parks and work the features to catch all the air and style buzz like our grommies have always wished for.

The creek's open terrain and numerous gullies stoke local hound dog freeriders like Andy G, who live to pop floaty crossbones down endless waves of runs like Wishing Well, Zig Zag and Ropers. If you're not a seasonal transplant, then you'd probably need a few visits to check out the entire Sun Valley side. Another playground of trees, creeks, wind lips and secret pockets of that epic crystal surface, wind shaped by the high plain conditions.

Mt Mackay holds some truly epic lines. Nice steep turns, lofty drops, rocks and natural kickers, all the way to the creek bed. It's seriously worth the hike out when the conditions are on. Dreaming the day it may become lift accessed? Keep your eyes open for Steve Lee and Tom Costa, doing back country touring, who love charge'n and sledin' the backside of Ruin Castle. The plank scene in the area has always been strong. On-par with everything to dig about H.C. The Costas, Moegels and van Puttens are true heartcore legends. Along with Laylor Lee and Brit Cox spreading the spirit to a new gen of girls. Stories about Mike Clarke (R.I.P.), Andy Mero and Eagle Pay - plus all the hot valley talent pump tons of progressive riding. it's epic! If you catch a glimpse of riders launching natural and man made jumps, it's probably the new gen with their air & style coaches doing their spinning and stomping dance. Be nice and they'll probably let you in on some mysteries of balance and stoke.

Hanging out around here can be tough though, which translates to expensive. If you're not in a lodge or on some sly work gig, do your supermarket shopping down the valley in Mt Beauty. It's cheaper and you can get a gourmet fix from the Bakery, Stock Pot or Swiss+Chips while you're being mesmerized by the Bogong views. Every season the food on the hill evolves. Gourmet from Fryers, Milch, Husky, ChopHouse or Elk keeps keep shredders happy. Or, hit the Pass or EasyEats for quick-chow. After riding find the après scene at any number of establishments and then stumble to one of the night spots. The village has a heart of gold and there's always fooz or pool to play. And the bands touring Horseshoe rock out too!

So what if H.C. and it's sister Mt H. are inhabited by a mixed bag of motley crew. It's these wild people living and riding every day (no matter where they're originally from or how ridiculous they act) who fuel the scene and give this place it's feel. Beneath all the expansion tactics and weekly tourism, this valley-end destination is filled with epic riding - period. More and more people are figuring it out, and heading on over to be a part of the scene. You know, to be Heartcore.

andy g - ski plus © Epic.

photo poetry by pea ce

All bow toward bogong, one mountain so strong - your storyteller on mt mackay - justin.

horseshoe GROOVE

At the crown
of this humble valley
lies a magical song
called Bogong
with a soul so beautiful
its light becomes a part of you
a spirit so strong
you can walk forever
and never be far from home
a knowing here or away
we can remain happy
work or play
a heart noble as the mountain
ladies and gentlemen
with energy like a fountain
the ones who school
experience their tool
truth the rule
warm to be cool

Whether we are hungry for our home hill
or lucky on travel, it's always easier
to look up riders in the know
and score *inside info!*

gibbo *with a spinning stalefish*

pea ce gully pow pow © justin

gibbo alcatraz © Epic.

The first time I saw a real *boardshop*
was like finding someone who cared
about our desire for balance
and quest for freedom
with gear in the shop
that shone like treasure
waiting for barter
on a warriors fight.
i licked my lips and
placed many wishes
saving the money
doing some dishes.

horseshoe
GROOVE

ben & troy @ MSC © Epic.

pea ce mt beauty sk8 park © justin

pea ce tweak © ray cruikshank

33

horseshoe GROOVE

nuey & slug **filming**

simon says **pipe style** © Epic.

What do you wish,
pipe jumping slug?
where you at,
cool ski-cat?
"can't get enough
sweet lovin fun!"

slug & eagle freeski © Epic.

slug lording bumps © tim lewis

Standing in the rat race sun
i dreamt a dream to have some fun
an extreme emotion this may seem
but in my heart it had to be
dreaming distant peaks of stone
covered with white substance known
for mad capos this place our goal
wanting with my heart & soul
to greet magnificence with thy eye
limitless grace thou shall fly
sliding on snow a worthy plan
greater than the falling sand
next thing knew, my heavy head flew
on wings of compassion start
sight gained upon mountain peak
beauty such my knees felt weak
Moments savoured never bleak,
fear aggression perfect flow
to realise something i didn't know
if ever in god I did believe
this was more than just a tease
content to watch the sun go down
leaving behind an ugly frown
sweet friends with good food
bounty of life for a perfect mood
within faith these hopes renewed
love to you heartcore crew.

simon 'slug' costa

pea ce ropers © justin

Jump rocks
children play
riding mountains
every day
Looking up
never down
laugh a lot
mr clown
Bird sing
dolphin swim
heartcore true
always grin.

pete lucas **mr clown**

pea ce le plunge © justin

ron dabu **ninja stiffy**

swindling **gibbo**

horseshoe GROOVE

drew gibson **style © Epic.**

Tail grab
powder burn
upside down
it's your turn
ride a board
all your life
skip old age
never die.

laif moegel *swiss travels* © Epic.

tom costa

Nomads at play
which way
which way
living by feeling
day after day
body follows mind
which follows heart
once at the end
we realise
it's just a start.

kylie petras

richie logan (r.i.p.) & amy gavin

ron dabu

shane lawther © cruzy suzzette

cover boy craig moegel © Epic.

It was an interesting season without any reason,
rainy at the start, how room mates fart
patience for storms, sweet powder horns
back to sun and melt, hailstone pelt
360's little flight, working all night
every possible shift, coin to travel nomad drift
jet airplane, back to winter again
different mountains, scenario the same
freeriding lady, you're so lovely.

horseshoe
GROOVE

horseshoe
GROOVE

Autumn red
heavy storm
cabin blue
powder cruise
spring sun
rainbow runs
summer call
winter colour.

classic clive

craig and ol'yella

ol'yella & cele

christian 'mario' mariethoz

craig and mario

pea ce slave to jah moegelski © Epic.

40

clive 'fyve' dickerson © Epic.

Body in tune
heart turned on
soul connected
all day long
riding park
is the way
tune your balance
the mountain way.

andy mero © *justin*

Chefs recipe for life
top quality ingredients
this is key
organic natural
real tast-ee
love and passion too
in everything you do
imagination willing to change
go with the flow moment-em
aim to please people true
heart and soul through
make happy all on earth
positive attitude always first
use the real love - one vibe
exciting life in every tribe
for dessert kick back relax
respect to those who believe
what is given shall be received
that's da word
in this here kitchen
cookin for you
sweet chilli drippin..!

sean oakley © *Epic.*

Ronnie the shred chef © *justin*

brent ' bumps' bignall © *justin*

horseshoe
GROOVE

mike clarke (r.i.p.) © justin

Powder powder everywhere Mike Clarke - chair air, local lads on international poma
bad boy corner copter. Snow bunnies waiting to bat, who will get who in the sack?
Don't scorn it's heaven's play, always in love the heartcore way.

nick 'eagle' pay © *justin*

Eagle Pay christened with style
by the simple grace
of going that extra mile
poetry in motion
hocus-pocus creation
balls on the line
hardly satisfied
never mind
he's a believer
in the limitless kind
beauty in nature
and a better world
by using less paper
folklore character
global chapter
papa now, happy ever after.

trent docking © justin   *amy gavin*

horseshoe
GROOVE

Places on Earth are outcomes of choice
even if they seem mysteriously subconscious
to reach the highest in everything we do
the dreams we make must be true
you are welcome to try another way
but when the snow comes, is it your day?

amy 540 © epic.

marky g © pea ce

A *freerider* feels the grind
to search moments of heart
moment to moment
every moment knowing
the excitement of living
is truly self producing

kat & AJ

serendipit soul

horseshoe
GROOVE

rob sarroff

living end © justin

Larger than life
crew who ride the night
rockin' the live music
and street light rails
hanging with the man
cause that's a fun plan
noisy of course
troublesome not at all
just a song of life
standing tall.

© Epic.

Justin sk8
Field design
photographic light
rainbow shine
cheers for the work
he's already given
enjoy this storybook
heart & soul driven

Summer come
mtn bike for fun
down hill dream
technical skill scene
animal forest play
rolling every day
keeping spirit fit
with a dirt dancing kit

horseshoe
GROOVE

big hill *mtn bike park*

andy mero *mt beauty © epic.*

When the day is done bikers balcony come
talking story true, tales exaggerated blue
of battle with the force, on mountain rocks of course
warrior wheels ok, will ride another day

Ninja heartcore jedi knight of the round table - Simon Costa - hangin' in a place he knows best © Epic.

Heartcore spirit

we are dedicated to epic balance
exhilaration for common good
friends awakening together
creating sacred form
tribes gather abundance
inspiring children born
adrenaline pumping action
deep fluffy slash dancing
epic terrain park play
river paddling oceans
surfing long lines to the beach
rolling wheels across concrete
rainbow lightning reach
magic chakra moments
Choosing karma rhyme
our truth flooding the land
free to enjoy special times
embracing heartfelt dreams
lifting all who feel alone
to realise we are together
incognito empath grow
navigating fear a big deal
bring us home to da heart
dancing people alive
warm in the big tree
all proceeds shared in our tribe
communities totally balanced
chirping bird song loud
ninja jedi skill sets
championing on a cloud
Robin Hood laughter
enlightened mind strong
noble warrior soul
forever kind with love

He skis with poetic style,
shies on corporate offers for sponsorship,
proudly risen above the best, plus fallen from injury,
discarding fear of poverty he steals hearts through cunning charm.
Tossing a lucrative signature ski deal he morphed into a back country tour guru...

How does Tom Costa do it?

Epic freeriders always deny that they are graceful, even though it is usually the most interesting thing about them. Nowadays, you can ask any seasoned rider, sponsored pro or modern hucker about their ability and their luck, and they will drone on about how unhappy/unpopular/unappealing they were when they began, insisting no one gives them a chance even now. Not far off the truth considering the most any Australian rider could ever hope out of sponsorship would be a dribble under their annual expenses.

So it is something of a relief to discover Tom Costa - whose talent and skill has shone through at numerous competitions, and who was voted, by peers, the skier most likely to lead the way - suffers none of these delusions. He has held out 'top five' clothing deals with loyalty and honour, while claiming he would be happy to ride for big labels if they talked less like painted slave traders. Tom is going to make it, just when and where? That is the question on our lips.

When I asked him at what stage he first became aware of his talent, he laughed. "I don't think I am there yet? I mean, I have always skied and what I can do must be relative to where I have been. Does that make sense?"

"Yes it does" I find my self answering, wishing I had skied from birth, and thus immediately dissing my ability to truly understand the depth Tom has with his sport. Just because I have been in the enviable position to ride with and witness such fluidity, style and awesome ability, the judgment will always remain with Tom.

CostaTom

Where did you grow up Tom?
Mostly in Falls Creek, our family travelled around a bit. We spent six months in Switzerland when I was about nine. That was pretty rad, we just skied every day and did school work at home in the evenings. Then my parents decided they wanted to stay in Europe. When they found a farmhouse in Italy they wanted to buy, my Mum returned to Australia to sell our flat in Falls Creek. If things had of turned out the way they had planned it I would probably be skiing for the Italian team, or farming somewhere in Northern Italy, but things didn't work out and we returned to Australia after a brief stint in England staying with my Mothers family. Since then I have been mostly in Falls Creek. But I haven't grown up yet!

So when did you start skiing and competing?
I started skiing when I was about 2 or something, and started going in races when I was about eight I guess. Then I went in the first Summit Masters back in 1985. Scored a few seconds in the Verbier Connection ski movie and got my photo in Powderhound.

And you've been in a few different teams?
Yeah. The first one was Team Green, which my dad started. He tried to get something going for all of the young locals in Falls. He took us all to the World Cup in Thredbo and organised for us to meet the great Alberto Tomba. I think we only really had the team for one season but it was definitely epic in its own way. After that Simon and myself joined up with other local rats Nick Pay, his cousin Sam and snowboarder Simon Flynn to form B.W.A. Influenced by gangster rap and sporting the brightest fluoro green and purple one piece suits available and we were styling. We rocked out in the fluoro for two seasons and Simon and I were both getting pretty good results in the mogul comps so we were upgraded to Team Red. These were pretty happy days, as members of Team Red we hooked up Quickie and Oakley sponsorships and I also started skiing on Salomon. But like all good things, that came to an end when the uniform sponsor decided to get out of teams and just keep only a couple of skiers. After that Ive been on the Australian Development Team, the Europa Cup Team, the World Cup Team and then in 99 there was the Salomon Freeride Team. Probably the first ski team in Australia to have both a phone company sponsorship and a dirty old VJ Valiant as a team car. That lasted one season and I was so broke at the end of it that I couldn't afford to take my spot on world cup.

So are you on any team now?
No, not really. I was on the world cup team for Australia last season but it didn't go very well and I'm not sure where I stand right now. I took some time out with injury and some friends of mine are thinking of starting a Centerlink ski team so maybe I will join them.

A life in the ski scene, what has changed?
I guess everything has changed a lot. When I started skiing it was cool and mogul skiing was cool. Then snowboarding came along and skiing wasn't so cool anymore. Now twin-tipped skis and freeriding have made skiing cool again. Its kind of funny to see people that used to ski then snowboarded and now there giving skiing a go again because its back in style, but whatever. I have always thought it was good fun and that's what it's all about. Apart from that there is the fashion, like I said we used to ski in fluoro green one-piece suits with headbands. Then there is the evolution of ski technology, largely influenced by snowboarding. This has been a huge change for skiing and has made skiing a more exciting sport. With twin tips and fat ass big mountain skis, skiers have been able to do things that were almost impossible ten years ago. I had never heard of a misty flip or D-spin until a few years ago. I remember watching Plake and Schmidt back in the day doing jump turns down chutes and stuff now you see guys bombing down Alaskan peaks at 100km/h outrunning avalanches and landing 15meter backflips off cliffs or busting all sorts of crazy ass spinning flips in parks and halfpipes.

And the business?
I don't know really. I am trying to educate myself on how this industry works but yet to work out how to get anyone to talk professionally. It is hard going and people don't realise that when they give us some free gear they are buying a lifetime of experience to promote their products. Too many people driving fancy cars and not sharing the loot. That is why I am giving the Force a go. When the production gets organised I will input design dreams and test prototypes. Then as the revolutionary shit that is happening rolls through I will actually get paid from sales commission. For sure all the bros will be riding them and Aussie riders will feel the benefit of local production.

So where do you see yourself in the future?
I see myself skiing somewhere in a far away place with deep powder and blue skies and luscious bowls and natural wind lips and oh, you mean seriously? I don't know exactly but I will be skiing. I want to do some more mogul comps and start trying more freeride style competitions and just have fun and enjoy my skiing.

And this year?
Just get switched on, work some moves out I have got in my head and model photos. I'm going to hang in Whistler a bit and when I come home go up and dance the Big Fella, I am looking forward to that. Bust out at some comp I suppose and just keep rolling the dice.

CostaTom

These tribal pages are designed to liberate our talented riders. *The noble warrior.* While celebrating the balance road and any realisation of our free spirit that lives and breaths across Earth.

Romain de Marchi - gateway to the sun © Epic.

Warrior heartcore jedi industry specialist, Timmy G, kindly hooking
us some scene. Pretty good for his first major mission since virginity.
Great work - very proud - the people are happier. Cheers bro!

SEE Life SIDEWAYS

Written from an ambition for balance and freedom, the visions in this storybook are dedicated to the spirit of our children. Let's connect and further develop epic balance strategies in culture. The aim of being heartcore is to see holistic recognition of balanced life. Creating abundance and purpose for action lifestyles.

Too many of our friends are misled to think there will come a time when they must stop riding, grow old and become an adult. Or if you are already an adult and old that it can't be turned around to rediscover some youthful happiness.

Epicscope believes this attitude is just clever drug and alcohol marketing by the slave driving illegalists. When we take the lies out of life, what we are left with are people who can stay true and use boardriding, or any form of balance, as a self examining act. To recognise the level of connection one is living with - whether or not one is going in the right direction? Physically, mentally and spiritually. We plan on shifting greedy ignorance by 100% profit sharing with the riders, writers and artists who have wished us into being and who will stand by this work because it comes from their heart. Courageously we will unite core balance scenes around the globe, some of which has already started, by pushing the development of epic balance centres - retreats, residences, schools with community action lifestyle choices.

Indoor / outdoor skate and bike parks with epic services to oil your bearings. Trampoline gyms. Ninja dojo coaching and nutrition. Climbing walls that lead to special hangouts. Offices where people work with supreme presence and efficiency (and play a lot). Air- tunnels for sky training. Rope swing aquatics. Icy plunge baths after steamy sauna sessions. Wave pools for mass surf stoke. Plus epic GTR (Geo Thermally Refrigerated) halfpipes for freestyle. Epic terrain. All environmentally sustainable. Designed, funded, constructed and maintained by the best, most skilled, connected and balanced people on Earth.

Massage affordable to the masses. Yoga & meditation spaces for daily practice. Natural organic food settings. Zen style rasta indigenous living. Generally - your standard Ninja Heartcore Jedi Knight Guru training facilities in every town, every city and every resort. Everybody enjoying an epic life! A world as one. Totally beautiful.

Pretty ideal hey? So we're giving it a go because we believe in possibility. If you also believe then get behind all heartcore people. Everything they create will be shared among the many, not the few. That means it's going to come back to you! Dream true and spread the positive vibe. Reach out to natures cry and let us know of places that we dream, so we can spread the wisdom.

Umgawa ;-)

art by travis garone urchin associates

SEE Life SIDEWAYS

mitch mckersey - 12 years young © epic

Little sk8 grommets
young wisdom old
heart and mind true
from times untold.
Tricks quietly solid
style smooth and kind,
salute humble warriors
giving sight to the blind.

fitzroy sk8 bowl - melbourne © epic

SEE Life SIDEWAYS

spyke buchanen ruling fitzy bowl

core park sk8ers

rippin' round da clock
dreams been working
more crew are stoked.
Tell all the kids
to come out and play
rolling wheels on ramps
is a bona fide way
to shred each day.

steve watson

warm ponds steve © epic

SEE Life SIDEWAYS

justin field Queenstown NZ © billy lance

Time riding boards
make gods of us all
practicing balance daily
is exercise for the soul
the ones who keep at it
get what they wish in life
learning the simple magic
that everything is choice.

paul hurley Wanaka NZ © justin field

mark neighbours Tairua © pea ce

nick kilderry fitzy bowl © justin field

SEE Life SIDEWAYS

mark neighbours on his home ramp © epic

Sometimes we travel
just for fun
meeting people
living as one
times may pass
memories live on
picture perfection
warrior strong.

mark neighbours at a hand made park in tairua © epic

SEE Life

Life time riders
swordsman true
balance kings of earth
vagrant nomads too.
If you see these rippers
poppin' smooth air
give'em our regards
& show'em you care.

Tim 'dorfus' McDougal (r.i.p.)

simon 'sac' reynolds © epic

west beach - radelaide

yurgen - @ renton's ramp in sunbury © epic.

SEE Life SIDEWAYS

richie brownfield elwood original -© epic

Skaters just skate
comparing tactics
while waiting their turn
to session lonely bowls
where only true grinders
can handle the gnarly walls.
when nobodies around
skaters just skate
raw balance their way
to purely create.

one eye chris © epic

one eye chris - fitzy long grind © justin

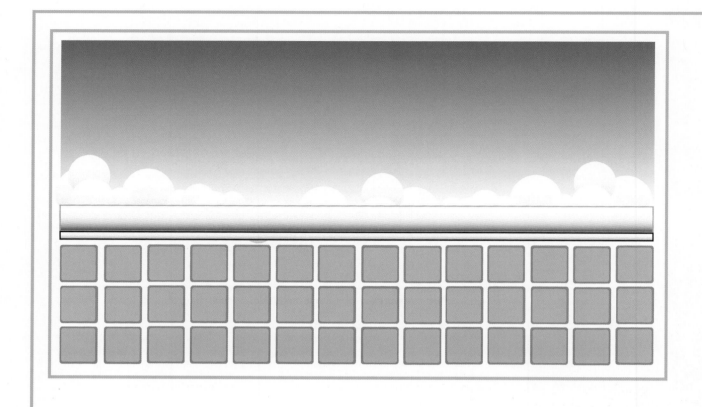

With all good things
our dreams will come true.
Sk8ing Richies pool
& laughing with the crew.
If you think we're crazy
simply wait and see
some are sk8ing with us
and some wont be.

blue tile fever - Richard Brownfield design

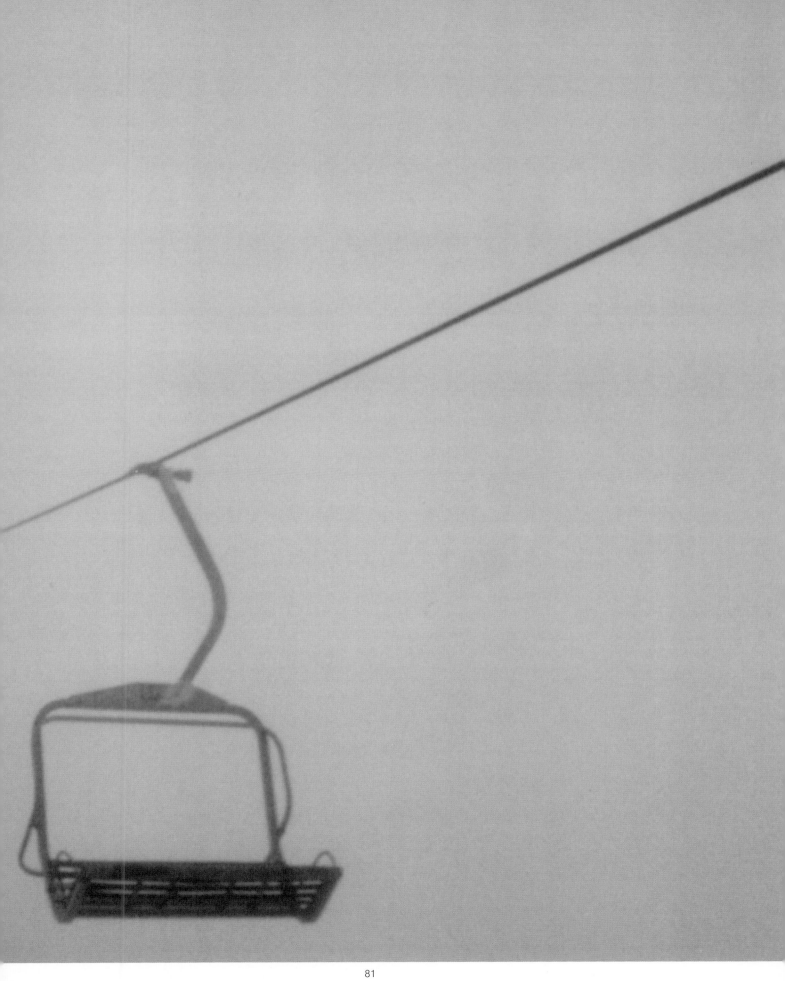

mount big-fog

Craig Mitchell - *Mt Buller Heartcore* - © *epic*

gibbo's crack at the jackpot

australian heart **from drew gibson**
dreamscape through **epicscope**

It started out
getting boozy
one afternoon
down Swindlers,
Hotham Central -
watering hole for the
hearty rich, benevolent
pilgrims and desperate
underworld freeriders
on a quest for the
endless winter.

The weather had closed in, so Jesse and I were brainstorming on how we were going to score a ticket North. Last year had swallowed our dwindling parental support for such dreams, and the Aussie alpine slave trade had served little justice to our O.S. fund. I felt unprepared and worried we would miss the season. For us hungry rookies that'd suck.

As we continued talking, I felt a tap on my shoulder. It was Ramon, a Hotham local, who congratulated me for winning the trip. "What trip?", I said in surprise. "The Big White trip" he replied, looking at me like I was a dumb ass. I had no idea what he was blabbing about until he spat the words 'Herbies' and 'jam night', not to mention how recklessly drunk I was that time. Then it clicked I had won the Big White trip for two to Canada.

Yeah, that's right! I'd won the end of season monster competition to Canada for two people, airfares, lift tickets, and accommodation - all worth $8000. So good! Unbelievable. I fell into shock. It was hard to take in. For once, I didn't have to stress - I was on the endless winter without fail.

Jesse scored the other slot on bro deal, and we agreed to consolidate our savings, loans and illegal earnings to buy a camper and allocate a petrol budget. We figured no matter where you spend a season, at sometime or another you'll get inspired to cruise to some other scenes. This way we could delete the rental expenses from our schedule and just follow storms at will.

gibbo's crack at the jackpot

We left the return air tickets open, and traded our accommodation for Big White season passes. It was sorted with launch date set for December 7. The only detail left was to score a Rocky Mountain passport, which would give us the option of ten resorts to call home throughout B.C and Western Alberta. We did that over the web with some more borrowed plastic and our adventure was sorted. December came like I was ten years old again. We flew into Kelowna early afternoon, where we were welcomed by Big White hosts and taken to the hill for free lunch and piss up. What more could you ask for?

A few days later we bought a classic Dodge Tradesman equipped with fridge, cooker, propane heater, table-to-bed workables and basically everything you need to survive. It was dirty and brown and leaked a little oil, but had pretty cool vibes going. Inside smelt like a bong house, so we named her the Brown Dutchman (thinking she'd had a bit of history) and moved straight in.

"...I felt a tap on my shoulder, it was Ramon, a Hotham local, who congratulated me for winning the trip."

We were set up and ready for endless road trips, but fairy tales aren't all fun and games. Faced with minus twenty celsius living discomforts, early injury, fear of poverty and the standard fish out-of-water paranoia panic sessions, we felt the bite of hard times.

At one stage, in a state of hopeless delirium, I wrote a refund letter for our rocky mountain passports so we could at least rent a warm room for the night. With no insurance, I conceded defeat knowing that our last days would be spent whining about the bullet proof fields of interior Canada, eating from trash cans, until we were found frozen dead in the morning light, cocooned by our beloved Brown Dutchman.

This only lasted until the coin was tossed and we demanded positivity from every situation. Then we met some really cool people whose friendships took us in. Times started changing. Riding became super fun, progressively rewarding and entertaining. The halfpipes were OK, we went on hikes, skated indoor parks and enjoyed hot showers after big share meals. The good times were rolling with no reports of better snow anywhere else.

Super pipes are the mission

Jesse Bateman is the chauffeur - *Gibbo is the bitch* © Epic.

"he hung up the phone saying,
'If you want epic times I'll see you here tonight'"

Jesse - Lake Louise © Epic.

gibbo's crack *at the jackpot*

When storm cycles finally started moving across the Rockies, we hit the road. Dreaming that eight hours north, in the Banff National Park, we would find big mountain deeps. Our passports (stoked we still had them) were pretty useful around Banff as Lake Louise, Norquay, Nakiska and Fortress were all welcoming us.

Jesse busted out pro style behind the wheel of the Dutchman for commendable amounts of time spent on the highway, just a month or so after officially receiving his licence. Since I haven't got my licence yet, I spent my entire cabin time plushed-out the back with my feet up studying magazines. Thanks bro.

Our first weather pattern didn't really cut it as the snow averaged on the poor side at these spots. Re-calculation on a day to day basis eventually sent us to Field, a small hippy town 30 km from The Lake, where Big Bird from Falls Creek had been living for 2 years. We didn't know where in Field he lived, but we were hoping to find him. Then he just walked right into us, claiming he'd moved but came back just to check his old mail. Amazing coincidence! I couldn't believe it.

We exchanged stories and followed him to his new house in Golden, 45 km west. His bros took us in, and we bought day tickets to ride Kickinghorse (formally called Whitetooth). Its resort size was doubled with a fat gondola that boasts some kick ass terrain and bullshit snow. One of the best freeride mountains I have seen. Lots of open bowls and chutes, crazy trees and a 12 km cat-track with constant hits and an almost perfect bank all the way down. Nobody knows about this place, which gave us lots of powder. Pigging pow for a week was awesome, but as soon as it was all tracked, we were craving it again.

After watching the weather channel and being constantly disappointed with no more snow forecasted, we had to move. So we highballed it down to Fernie, since it's on our passport and Jesse's brother was hanging there. We couldn't believe our eyes as we entered the village to see a nice looking Terrain Park and Pipe.

The crew took us riding that afternoon, super-stoked cause the famous Siberia Bowl opened for the first time all season. A consistently steep forest with well spaced trees and some gnarly exits to get you back to the Whitepass Chair, definitely worth the five-minute hike. We bombed it a few times each and headed back to the van for food and sleep.

These times were rad, but yet again no new snow and none forecasted for another week or more. What the hell is going on? It's early February and Fernie is lucky to have over 150cm. We did have some good days in the untracked back country, but mostly rode pipe for those three weeks.

Then one night out of the blue, it started dumping huge flakes, building up an inch an hour. Filth! At around 11:00pm our friend Luke phoned Andy's house from Whitewater, going on about all this snow they had and how the storm was holding for a few days. He hung up the phone saying, "If you want epic times I'll see you here tonight".

Jesse and I were hanging to hit the Fernie lines we'd scoped, but there was a chance the storm centre wouldn't make it this far, so we took the offer. Whitewater with 40cm of fresh and a major dump hooking in, who could refuse? Four hours later we met Luke in Nelson, 15km from our next epic session. By 3.30am we had crashed to wake early all amped for the uncrowded powder runs in store for us. The van struggled up the hill until the ice and snow won, so we parked it and hitch hiked.

Once there, the word in line was "all-time". We rode the summit chair to the top and bombed straight down. Sick terrain everywhere deep with POW. The local knowledge served us sensationally. Backside lines so sweet, with long ass runs taking you to the road where we hitched back up. You can go 2km down the road or 10km, it's up to you, definitely one of my favourite runs ever.

The next day was a blue bird and we scored more epic snowboarding doing the usual hitch trick. On a lift back up the hill I spotted a nice log slide off the road with a drop at the end onto a bank. Perfect sunny conditions made this an arvo to remember. Jibbin in the sun is rad. I love it. The next day was hardcore hiking White Queen, a moderately steep open face with pillows, tree chutes and booters. It took just over an hour to reach the top. After a well deserved rest we bombed it, getting face shots nearly every turn. We were spent having scored big time.

Cody Bateman - Fernie pillow drop

Hiking the super pipe at Lake Louise © Epic.

gibbo's crack at the jackpot

Totally stoked, we regrouped at Luke's house for a stretch and feast. Recharging our batteries. The next day involved a little hike to a 30-foot cliff with a nice open landings. We all dropped it a few times then took a sweet tree run back to the day lodge.

Then it was back to Fernie, hoping there would still be some fresh around. Lucky for us there was. Once we totally shredded the remaining pow, it was halfpipe time. The pipe wasn't maintained well, but whatever, any air is good air. After two full-on days in the pipe we decided to check out Kimberley and Panorama on our way back to Golden. Panorama had an almost perfect set up with pipe & park both under lights and pumping tunes. This was total heaven.

Lucky for us, it was Friday and night riding was on. We literally got our snowboard gear on and piss bolted up the hill to the pipe. A small but fun pipe to ride made it the perfect session. We had been on the road for hours and a little stiff legged. I was struggling with kinks in the transition and decided to hit up the park instead. Which turned out to be a good choice as I was riding jumps and jibs better. A few nice moves with no slams always makes you feel good.

We deserved a few beers and hit the van to rest up for tomorrow's session. Jesse fell sick the next morning and didn't ride so I went out solo to explore the mountain. It was a big area with lots of potential, but the lack of snow made it hard to ride some of the gnarlier stuff. I ended back at the park. When I returned to the van Jesse was getting ready to leave for Big Bird's place.

Returning to Field, it started snowing really heavily and the road was getting dodgy. Little did we care cause we were in for more pow. Driving through heavy snow gave us rolling giggles. Driving into the Rockies there were howling winds and lots of fresh snow blowing around. We were stoked. So stoked in fact we pretty much drove straight to the Lake so we would be there when we woke. Hungry for some epic goodness.

Due to the storm strength on the Rockies, the heavy falls we drove through were patchy and elusive. It didn't dump everywhere. We woke to a clearing super-pipe day that worked us pretty hard due to the icy walls. I took some slappers in the park too and even though the next day was sunny, it was another heavy high-pressure session. Luckily it wouldn't be long till we scored fresh again.

Gibbo 180 lip slide 360 out on the mini pipe at Panorama

90

"super-pipe!"

Drew Gibson - frontside boost © Epic.

gibbo's crack at the jackpot

What an epic winning streak!
The very best of Fernie BC
Drew Gibson © Epic.

The next grey goose led us up to Marmot Basin early enough to score some good ol' fresh. It had snowed again almost as evidence our dream was an evolving reality. Life is rad when it rolls moment to moment. Although some lessons were dealt, everything seemed like it was mysteriously planned. Deep snow in open bowls which reminded us of New Zealand, plus some tight trees and laughable times.

After Marmot Basin we were back on the road, eventually hooking some work for cash & food (underground style) to set up more road time. Once the weather started moving again, it was another drive through Nelson and back to Fernie hoping something was lurking in the skies ready to dump anytime. That it did, probably thanks to our good mate Bondy who was hitching with us. He's one of those dudes that usually brings snow with him. Crazy lines went down the next morning, knee-deep in fact, and being at Fernie where it's steep with mad terrain everywhere – we were in heaven yet again.

Next night it dumped like I had never seen it dump before. We pig snorted the most epic morning of our lives, then drove nine hours to Kelowna to pick up PeaCe, who was joining us for a few weeks to shoot this story. We ditched Bondy on the road to Whistler and headed straight back to Fernie telling Pete how epic it was. I couldn't stop raving and thought I'd trip the dude out, but he's hot on the buzz and was into everything going on.

By 10am we were back and straight into the goods again. It was filth, PeaCe was loving it and I was too. Jesse was ripping and we just fed off each other. The day ended with the usual gourmet cook up and an early night cause it looked like the sun would shine.

Perfect skies and bombing action up top woke us with fat smiles. The program was for photos all day so we headed up and waited for the new lines to open up. When it did, it was standard ski bum chaos and we were loving it. We pulled up to hike a windy and got busted by patrol for being literally metres outside a closed sign. They were narky as, mostly because we made them miss a few fresh turns. Our passes were snatched, but since we were promoting the area, they showed some warmth and asked us to sit an avalanche exam before they were returned.

They skied off and we decided to build a hit somewhere on our way down. We spotted a nice wind lip that sent you over a set of small trees and onto a perfect landing. After shaping, we sessioned it for an hour or so. Before entering the village we hit the new park that was built for a slope style comp a few weeks earlier. It was small and didn't really give you a nice floaty air, so it was back to the van before our avalanche test.

Another roadie was under way and Panorama was the next call for a night session in the pipe. The conditions were icy but that didn't bother Jess, who busted some nice solid airs.

gibbo's crack at the jackpot

"...being at Fernie where it's steep with mad terrain everywhere – we were in heaven yet again..."

jesse 'the chauffeur' bateman © epic.

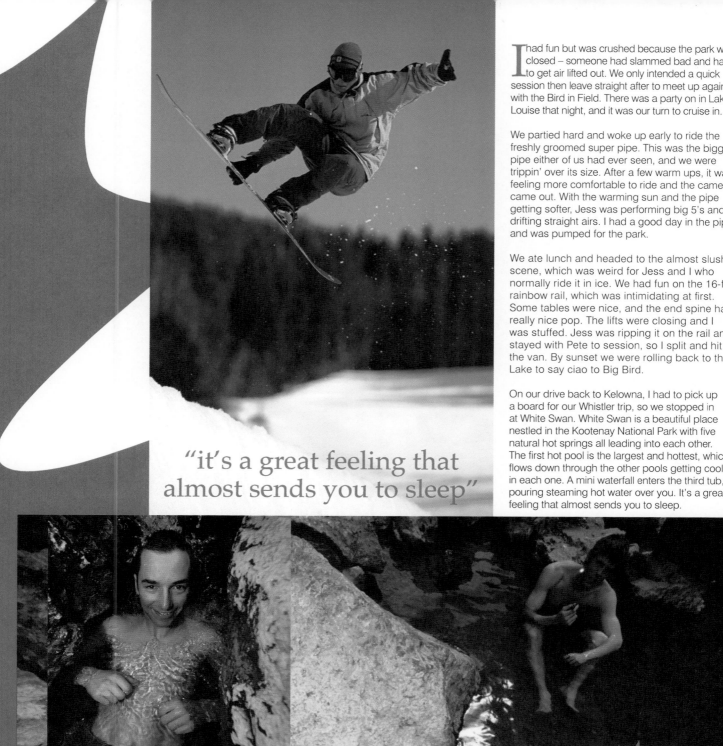

I had fun but was crushed because the park was closed – someone had slammed bad and had to get air lifted out. We only intended a quick session then leave straight after to meet up again with the Bird in Field. There was a party on in Lake Louise that night, and it was our turn to cruise in.

We partied hard and woke up early to ride the freshly groomed super pipe. This was the biggest pipe either of us had ever seen, and we were trippin' over its size. After a few warm ups, it was feeling more comfortable to ride and the camera came out. With the warming sun and the pipe getting softer, Jess was performing big 5's and drifting straight airs. I had a good day in the pipe and was pumped for the park.

We ate lunch and headed to the almost slushy scene, which was weird for Jess and I who normally ride it in ice. We had fun on the 16-foot rainbow rail, which was intimidating at first. Some tables were nice, and the end spine had really nice pop. The lifts were closing and I was stuffed. Jess was ripping it on the rail and stayed with Pete to session, so I split and hit the van. By sunset we were rolling back to the Lake to say ciao to Big Bird.

On our drive back to Kelowna, I had to pick up a board for our Whistler trip, so we stopped in at White Swan. White Swan is a beautiful place nestled in the Kootenay National Park with five natural hot springs all leading into each other. The first hot pool is the largest and hottest, which flows down through the other pools getting cooler in each one. A mini waterfall enters the third tub, pouring steaming hot water over you. It's a great feeling that almost sends you to sleep.

"it's a great feeling that almost sends you to sleep"

gibbo's crack at the jackpot

Jonas Emery © Epic.

We got to Whistler the next afternoon where the village was alive. The World Snowboarding Championships were on, and all the best riders on Earth were there to win an incredible US$250,000 in combined prize money. The slope style was incredible with the likes of Kevin Jones, Todd Richards, Jussi and many others there to put on a show. The tables were huge with amazing kickers and landings. A few rails were thrown in and at the end stood the biggest quarter pipe I have ever seen. It would easily reach the top of a three-storey building.

Guys were ruling it – JP did the biggest Mc Twist on the quarter pleasing everyone. In the end Todd won, followed by KJ and Jussi. The Jib Jam was sick with Marc Frank, Kevin Jones, JP walker, Andrew Crawford, Jeremy Jones, Chris Englesman and others performing on some crazy rails including a rainbow which went over water.

First place was a new motor bike, which Kevin Jones took home after pulling off a f/s 450 to rail. Chris Englesman came second with some super-tech styley boardslide transfers to f/s boardslides.

The super pipe finals were held the next day where riders were blowing spectators minds, including mine as they punched it down the perfectly groomed pipe. Kier Dillon was a stand out busting 15-foot McTwists and landing perfectly into trannie. Jonas Emery was ripping with his huge f/s 7's and 9's. Hardingham was going massive. All the riders were amazing to watch. Ross Powers took first place earning him a nice US$20,000.

That night was the big air. Set up in the heart of Whistler Village, a huge table top, stage and thousands of people was a breath taking sight. Yet again riders impressed. Kevin Jones f/s 1080s spectacular, not to mention Jussi's performance. It was epic and everyone enjoyed them selves.

Gibbo style circa 2001 © epic.

The whole event was unbelievable. The next morning wasn't easy getting up due to our hangovers from the end of the festival parties, but we managed. It was a dull day with 7cm of fresh and not many people out, which was unusual for a Sunday. We rode Whistler, which is such a Mecca.

I wasn't feeling too well, so I took a few more runs and went in while Jess and Pete stayed out still looking for a nice untouched section. That arvo, the Alpine Meadows hot tub was calling. It was Pete's last night in Canada and we'd pulled it off. Things were so awesome. The season was winding up and we made the absolute most out of it. I did my first pro work as a rider and met all my heroes who showed me how human and cool they are and that we all have the ingredients to make it. Travel experience is so good for you. I just love it.

The next two weeks consisted of skating and waiting to skate as it rained quite a bit. We were flat out of money and had to sell the van before we left Whistler. This happened twenty minutes before boarding our bus to the Slam City Jam. The Brown Dutchman lives on. We had cash and were going to see the best street and vert skaters in the world putting on their show.

The season for Jess and I ended perfect. The snow across Canada wasn't up to reputation, but we nailed her down. We followed the storms and avoided most slumps. Looked for perfect pipes and found them. Rode big parks and basically went where we wanted to go. We looked up resort websites, called friends, and sussed out our shit so we would be straight to score the goods. We made some mistakes and learned from them. That's the beauty of dream living - do it cause you know you can, that's what I'll be telling all the bros. See you on a mountain some time.

Kier Dillon
Rick McCrank

gibbo's crack *at the jackpot*

Many thanks to Lake Louise for refunding our Rocky Mountain passports, hope you enjoy the promo. And also to all the crew at Whistler, who hooked us up to meet the pros. Plus Herbies, for putting on sick raffles and not screwing us on it. Of course K2 for the free sticks, how's the pro gig look'n dudes? Oh yeah, and the old man for the loans, you know I'll pay ya back. Cool. Catch-ya.

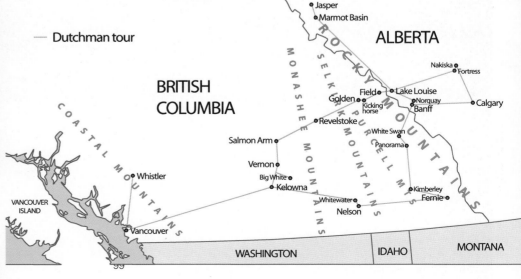

— Dutchman tour

Todd Richards campagning an epic Whistler super pipe © Epic.

Sitting in a Swiss chalet with a bung knee gives me time to contemplate my position. It's only a matter of days before I'm sliding again. More to the point, before I'm back in therapy. Injury is therapy too, teaching me to reach a higher connection with my abilities. But riding is the best therapy. The act of snowboarding is rewardingly nutritious for ones mental and physical well being. From the affect of the naturally beautiful surroundings to the adrenalin filled action of riding, this experience is individually soulful. As a form of expression, the sideways glide is my driving force to continue such a lifestyle. I guess it's why many people worldwide are doing the same thing. Living for the ride. Making sure they are in the right spot at the right time, when it's happening. Scoring epic days each season through years of dedication.

Memories of my endeavours are so vivid, the snow conditions, the friends I've had the pleasure of riding with, the different scenarios we encounter in the mountains, and just the feeling of freedom. The Alpine experience even appears in my dreams. I can clearly remember a chairlift ride I had in dream land. The chair was a two seater and with me was a friend from FallsCreek, Ol'Yella as many know him. We were definitely OS, due to the massive peaks which surrounded us and the quantity of virgin pow on the ground. I don't recall the conversation, however I do remember the feeling of absolute titillation that this chair was taking us to the top.

In the dream we never reached the top and I never rode that terrain. But this year (two years after the dream), Ol'Yella came to visit Switzerland and I caught up with him in Nendaz. Where, for the first time on foreign ground, we rode together. The day was awesome. With two Swiss bros we tracked some nice lines, although it wasn't quite a connection to this dream. After enticing him to session our secret spot on the other side of Valais, we headed for Leysin to say g'day to some mates working on the world series. When we arrived an attractive storm had rolled in. So we hung out for just over 24hrs hanging out in rasta style bars. The night before the half pipe finals it was seriously puking its tits off. From within I could sense that feeling of titillation.

We rose early the next morning. Still snowing with about 50cm of super fluffy pow on the balcony of our squat. The stoke of how much could have fallen on top was feverish. Ol'Yella and I would be the only two freeriding, as the others had to remove snow from the pipe. Poor bastards. 'Cause unbeknown to us, the day ahead was to be an epic adventure in both our lives.

The purchase of a day ticket can be calculated by how many mind blowing face shots you can get on a powder day like this. Say five bucks a face shot (cheap cause we're ski bums). That means anymore than ten epic blinders and it's a good deal. No worries. I was ready to go on the plastic for this one. Then something rather unusual happened. I'm still baffled by what went down at the ticket box except that Ol'Yella attempted to buy two tickets with a $100 Australian, which wasn't an issue. But when the girl came back after checking the exchange rate, she printed up one ticket and handed back 40 Swiss francs as change (the exchange rate being nearly 1:1). Confused, Ol'Yella repeated his request for two

tickets. And realising her mistake the girl printed another ticket and, almost giving him 90 francs more, handed over another 30. With grins now exploding we walked, rather quickly, from the counter with two(60 franc a piece) day tickets for only 30 bucks! Ol'Yella kindly gestured, as we entered the telecabine, "This one's on me mate."

We arrived at the top and I'm telling ya - it was bullshit! Riding from the piste into a ledge of snow, leading to the steep, was blinding. The powder being so light it barely floated my board. For a second I thought I was the deepest anybody could possibly get when Ol'Yella, on ski's, ploughed by hooting and munching, even deeper still. The colour of his goggles and beanie were the only recognisable features. My first ten turns were the ten most epic, all-time, face shots I've ever had. Opportunity well spent. The day continued like this until we could no longer ride from sheer exhaustion and the fear of overdose. Plus a world cup pipe comp was nearly over and I personally wanted to have a look.

It was during our powder munching sessions that I scored a moment of rare clarity. We had worked our way across the entire resort, from one chair to the next. And while sitting in silence as we rode a two seater, over virgin pow, surrounded by amazing peaks, mostly blanketed in cloud, I experienced déjà vu. That feeling of titillation rocketed to it's peak and I started giggling just because we were headed for the top. Flash backs of the dream came flooding in. I was almost ready to tell my friend of the dream and it's relevance to this situation, when he grinned and said "This has to be the best snow I've ever had in my life, ha ha ha..." All I could do was scream laughter and raise my hands in the air. This was it. An epic day that will remain in my head till I die, like many other times. I'm not really up with all the good advice in the world. Sure some people say get a real job and you'll succeed. But if you want to do something different then go right ahead. Because if you're happy, you've succeeded already.

I recommend ploughing through ice cold crystals of H2O, munching a little as you go. It's just something fun to do, no more, no less. You wont experience anything like it because of the unique quality it has to please the mind, body and soul. The sight of falling snow is nothing like rain or hail. Snow brings a calmness to an area, gently blanketing everything it settles on. Connecting each crystal is the work of gravity and the wind. And thanks to the sun, the snow eventually melts and returns down the streams, into the rivers and back to our oceans. We are at mother natures call. We sometimes wait, prey to her often and bless her when she delivers. She is the sweetest gem we can cherish, the purist force that can feed us. Ride, live, learn and be merry.

Memories to me, like dreams, are important. Days like I described don't need photos, sure we could have snapped the best shots of the season. But what we did was listen to mother nature who was telling us to ride and enjoy. Simple signs like the lift tickets, those tracks we instinctively followed to naturally majestic terrain, with the finest of bottomless snow, are everything in life. The ear to ear grin comes back on every recollection. No doubt when I see Ol'Yella again we'll recall that joint adventure. And hopefully feel that amazing experience of titillation again.

story by nick mcnally

DEEP

christophe margot photography

Nick McNally living the dream in Switzerland © Epic.

pea ce by nuey

POETIC SURF

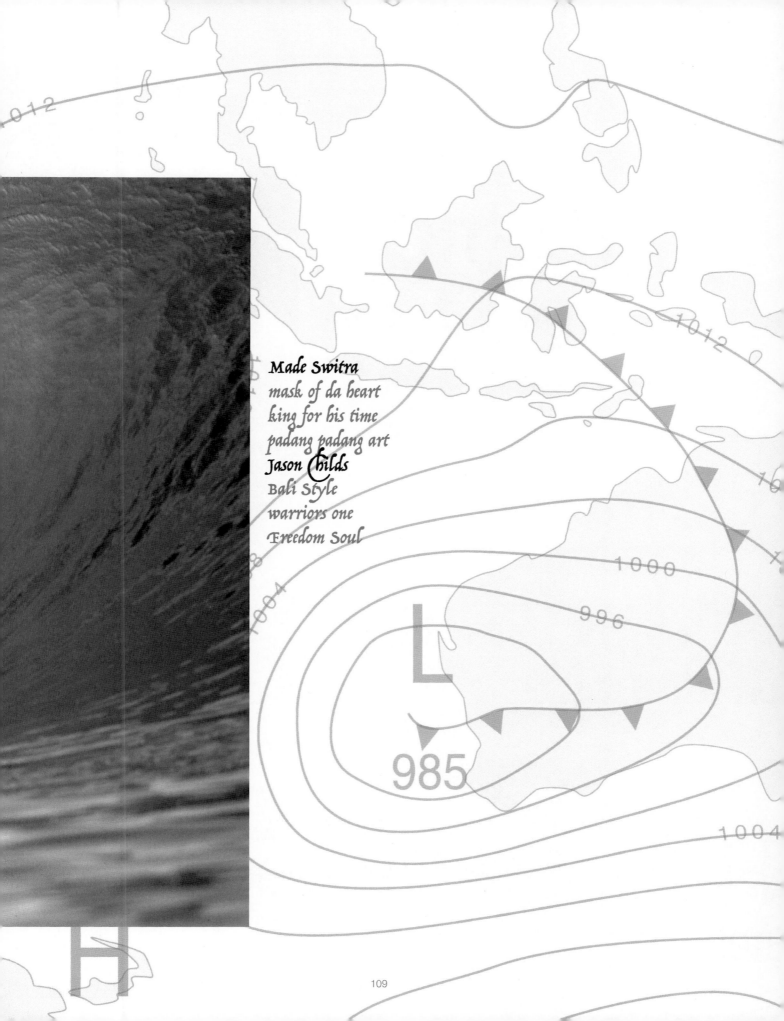

Made Switra
*mask of da heart
king for his time
padang padang art*
Jason Childs
*Bali Style
warriors one
Freedom Soul*

POETIC SURF

Fresh outta da barrel
straight off the boat
green room imagery
purely for stoke
don't just look
feel the vibe too
freeride life
  for every surfer true

surf photos courtesy of the mosquito warrior Jason Childs

Dylan Longbottom
billabong crew
working class hero
Indonesian tubes
this is the life
salt sun sand
crystal blue water
warrior stand

Paul Gurteen photo - Taupo NZ

Ninja heartcore jedi freeflyers - jk & sky dingo - prepare for some more earth leakage.

Earth leak soul speak, head down free fly,
get on it any way you can, happy times jumpin' from planes

Earth Leakage freefly movement

Fly through the air on a wing and a prayer
overcoming your fear in the troposphere
timeless power feelings a buzz
soar mr eagle heavens above

© Mark McCaulgan photos

rising light · switzerland © Epic.

Sven Mermod knows his backyard like a Jedi knows the force - epic Les Diablerets

It's mid morning, midweek...

surrounded by sky-piercing peaks. Soft French Reggae leaks from two speaker boxes, located either side of a postcard view from our new alpine abode. Inspiration floats around the room as snow continues to fall outside. Thick cold snow. Just four days until this little known, better kept secret, resort opens it's lifts for the season. One chair, six button tows, a T-bar, and the most unbelievably insane terrain anywhere in Valais.

the big O' - Valais Suisse © Epic.

shhh... this spot's a secret

Cyril Neri © Epic.

shhh... this spot's a secret

No, I can't tell you where, exactly. Even though I should under my "free-ride" agreement. Because it's too damn good and I, for one, am not yet void of selfishness. If the word gets out we all know exactly what will happen. Mass exodus of the filthy rich, unreasonable price rises, fat lift queues and less fresh tracks. Hard to get fresh tracks. Fark that.

Sorry, but we've already hiked a high alpine cabin and observed the sheer epicness of this area. Slashed some all-time face shots, down crazy lines. Scored perfect powder. Witnessing, on our finger tips, some of the most mind blowing ride potential any freerider could possibly dream about. Limited lift capacity means powder lasts. Resort designers with soul, a seeming lack of greed, or just kind hearted mountain folk.

A vast contrast to maxed out areas such as Whistler in Canada, Verbier across the Valley, or Chamonix just over the border - where if you're not in line hours before first lift after each storm, then you may well miss out on riding untracked virgin pow, at most, having to rush for it.

Not in this place, shhh... this secret spot has the kind of resort attitude which rewards it's visitors. Pure freeriders & valley locals who live, search and know the feeling. Some of you reading this may well know what I'm talking about.

Freeride friends - Doc, Milon and the Marmot © Epic.

Lucky Sven

On location again... This time shacked up in a prejudice-free Wallis (if you speak Swiss-German) residence, or should I say - comfortable three bedroom Chalet. Just 24 hours from my sun burnt upbringing. With Cyril 'Doc' Neri, Sven 'Marmot' Mermod and Olivier 'Milon' Favre. Three of the most respected and jaw achingly funny rasta spirited free souls this country has ever produced. Some snowboarders and a skier - good name for a movie. Friends. Freeriders. Balance professionals.

Besides this trio, I share my blissful morning experience with Nick 'Nuey' McNally. Partner in crime, Falls Creek bro and self-confessed fear-addicted, unaccomplished snowboarder/ artist. Who actually oozes more natural style than just about anyone I know.

Nuey is sunken into the couch busting back to back cab 900 grabs and multiple kick flip grinds on Tony Hawk's Pro Skateboarder play station. Which, incidentally, has become the ultimate cabin fever medicine for every dedicated freedom hunter worldwide.

In the background an old Toko iron smoulders. Filling the air with a smell of performance from pre-session tuning. In font, our European connection are working out some sort of high tech electronic muscle pumping gadget. With electrodes stuck onto their bare legs which pulsate fibrillating shocks to and fro (like something Aliens would use on ones temples for brain washing). Making them sweat and cringe in a scientifically proven attempt to tone their riding power before the end of this big storm.

123

shhh... this spot's a secret

A season starter, which is said to dump waist deep powder before the sun returns to warm our vision. So the predictions go and at this rate - with 90cm of snow base here already, plus a fresh foot on the balcony - actually sounds quite believable.

The music continues. Helping each member of this recently assembled family meditate on their exact living purpose. Part of which is to ride big-ass, statistically dangerous, ancient and wondrous mountain tops. Preferably in view of a camera, at least some of the time. Yet another winter in the freezing cold, amongst jagged peaks over flowing with undiscovered lines, minimal nightlife and probably even less single free loving women - shall be a healthy challenge.

So we'll have to hike a little - pack peeps, probes, shovels and hope our time doesn't come yet. On a weekly basis. No doubt masturbate and run up visa bills to survive in such an expensive, linguistically difficult culture. Deep into stoke! Closer to source.

Three weeks with Jah... a dark solstice is upon us. Fuck the sceptics. This negative mental crap ain't going to last. We've been tit deep in the goods, cold giggling, surf slashing, plume producing, rock dropping, bottomless bouncing, powder-cart-wheeling, stoke living and as self absorbed as ever.

God damn freeriders. Lazy pricks. Due mainly to our lack of work and maximum playtime. You see, we ain't part of no slave trade. We've been assembled to build a snow park, maintain it, and stoke out some tourists in the process. Sounds like such a cool job hey? But it gets better...

This secret spot, part of the Muveran Massif and just over the horizon from Les Diablerets, has only a hand full of snow grooming machines (you know, low budget) and due to the large accessed area, subsequent long pistes, coupled with unusually huge snowfalls - it takes two or three days grooming before any driver is allowed to push jumps around for us. Powder before parks. Good concept.

pea ce © nuey

shhh... this spot's a secret

peace © nuey

This all means that we need not turn up for work after it snows more than 30cm. Seems a pity. Except the snowfalls so far have been fifty plus! Shockingly perfect because this is the first job, I've had being a snow bum, that let's me happily freeride every single epic day.

Since our first shovel session it has rained a little, and then dumped another meter. We pigged it, of course. And just when we thought we'd create some more custom air time (work that is) it's dumping again. Wouldn't you know it - no machine. Such a shame. But I suppose that if there are freeriders somewhere that want to ride parks before powder - good luck to 'em.

shhh... this spot's a secret

peace © nuey

"...this is the first job, I've ever had being a snow bum, that let's me happily freeride every single epic day..!"

Wiamea size lip slash, style'n with Sven © Epic.

Sven Mermod. *Freedom trees* © Epic.

Personally I'm not recommending they expand the grooming fleet here. Because at this rate we'll be licking the silver spoon long into this season and wont have to work till near spring. Which is OK as our accommodation comes complimentary from the boss and our staff pass gets us unlimited use of the thermal baths, for which this destination is famous. Ahh..., relaxation. If I have to, I'll eat rubbish for times like this. Starve. No problem.

It sounds like a fantasy huh? Maybe I'm painting white lies, like us Australian bastards are renowned. Spinning a web of make believe. Well, let me say one thing to you my friend, as I whisper in to your ear, "heaven is mostly a state of mind" I hate hell. Despise negativity. And this place, shhh... this no bullshit secret spot, is not free of such devious activity. Story of the 20th century.

It's holiday time. Fiesta Noel. And with it comes good business for the Man. Plus some very stupid humans from all parts of the world. I have pity for these people because they might have discovered such a destination, but most of them just don't see the best it has to offer - happiness. And that could be as simple as positive thinking?

The peak hour fact... which to some may not be ideal, I suppose will happen every school break, public holiday or fresh snow weekend for the rest of the winter. Half hour waiting for the chair, ten or twenty minute queues on the drags. Early mornings if you wish to session glory lines. People with straight faces, unhealthy bodies, maybe stagnant thoughts. All the while I jump up and down - hyperactive and giggly. Hustling and snaking inconspicuously like James Bond on a mission, to the front, to the top for more. Because I'm just so in love with life, with riding Swiss powder.

shhh... this spot's a secret

Another thing I've discovered - nobody else is carrying rackets. Good on'em. Cause to us freeriders, that's the key to tolerating crowds. Spend a little more time finding the lines you like. Don't rush'em, session'em. Simple.

Study the clues, come to heaven... and "feast your beady eyes on these lines!" Cyril exclaimed, cutting a wooded ridge leading into a quadruple staircase avalanche billabong that we later named 'balconies'. Pulling out the extreme scope, bred from big mountain experience, he stares down the beast in to a zen like state.

Above head pillows and layered drifts (resembling sandstone cliffs at the beach), line it's walls. Begging you in from the beauty. Bringing on fear from a mind boggling amount of snow - drowned rocks ? "C'est magnifique les gars!" he screams, froth spitting from his mouth.

Almost a wild animal soaked deep into it's hunt. Ready to kill. "Sixty degrees in!" he's anxious, scanning lines, "And the bottom looks so good from here!.." he's seriously considering the snake. Then with a slight pause and our confirmation -"it's all good!" - drops straight in. "Yippee!"

Accelerating warp speed twenty six, smoke stacks pillowing skyward. Tight, relaxed stance. Disappearing, reappearing. Pealing left, cranking right. Signature simmer slashes. Sven was close after, from my right. "I & I, rasta-far-i". His approval accompanied by that distinct 'marmot' chuckle. No turns, just a straight path of destruction. Trying to keep his head out like a periscope. Up the other side Sven rockets into the air. A burley slow motion transfer that devastates the pillowy soft landing some distance down below. Freight training. Not a hiccup - phenomenal.

shhh... this spot's a secret

test pilot nuey © pea œ

Cyril soul arc © Epic.

pea ce balcony charge © nuey

shhh... this spot's a secret

Already Nuey and Milon are screaming! I can't see them but their double jacking plumes just add to the chaos. I'm such a dreamer, still standing a top and stoke'n on everyone else. It's my turn. My own inner glory like living in a movie, I never want to leave. There was almost sex at the bottom. Not quite but hugs and high fives and ear touching smiles between us all. Laughter. Remembrance. This is boardriding. This, my long lost friend, is freeriding... with some mates... in a place I call heaven.

At the bottom Cyril gives some direction for our next run. "We take the top T-bar and then session it back. Except we must keep our speed full power to glide above the canyon and into a forbidden zone. This is an avalanche path so don't mess around, move silently fast. Once you round the ridge simply spot the Indian Chief (a big wise tree) and hold your line high. When the mountain splits in three, take the most attractive gully. They're all good, but only one rider at a time.

This is my special place. A secret shared with you dear friend. And when you're turning please let the mountain rejoice in your smile. Then peel right above the river until you reach the ridge above our snow park. Here I will wait for you or you can wait for me and after some air time we can do it again." Absolutely epic.

Remember that it's all good, riding the experience of travel. The house of love as our guardian. I've just enough time to re-wax, ride again and come back to an all night party. Even more snow. Wonder if things are that different tomorrow, in another century? In any case, when my old mates started counting down their last seconds before that moment, back home in Melbourne (at 1.59:50pm, Swiss time)

I was slashing over head roosters at 6000ft. Minus ten. Belly deep. Secretly missing every single one of them and pondering to myself "Why people don't realise possibility?"

Get it right... heaven is a state of mind, a course of action. There's no need to reveal the name of where we're at. If you search, you will find. If you travel, you will get richer. There are universal laws. So we've grown to kings from peasants. The production of liberty, honour and stoke in practice. Not so much where you are at, but who is the spirit inside your heart? That, after a point, is just our choice. And that, my friend, is known as real freedom.

So practice control over the forces that get you to where and who you want to be - your thoughts. The power of your mind. Don't loose or abuse it. Don't even let it sleep too long. Take a hold of it. Study it. Have fun with it. And then you'll become a freerider. You'll finally know the feeling of epic freeriding. Thanks for coming!

shhh... this spot's a secret

Poetic Ladies

Anne-flore Marxer *HMH Wanaka NZ* © Epic.

Andrea Binning *freeski Chamonix* © Xandi Kreuzeder

138

Yvette Craig © Mike Truelove

Freedom is free
riding your board
be open and kind
to find your line
for peace of mind.
Pressure subsides
climbing so high
wind in your hair
freedom is the vibe.
This is your time
do what you must
speed is our friend
in skills we trust.
To all the girls
who have the desire
what's inside you
is all that's required.
Ride strong, fly high
and you will find
your true freeride.

Very

sufing the Earth

artists at work

Nicolas Vaudroz © Epic.

Nicolas Vaudroz was my idol the very first time we met. I had no idea who he was, never seen him ride, and if I let my upbringing regurgitate some judgement - I would have said at a glance that he seemed a bit nerdy. But he was my idol none the less, for the simple fact he was a full-time park-building cat driver. A concept rudely rejected at home before the pro-park revolution.

We met in Switzerland last century, to shape glacier pipes. So that riders, including myself, could study the rudimentary logistics of weightless balance. Nicolas was our machine operator and I was part of a tight-nit hand tuning squad. Halfpipes in snowboarding are an unquenchable thirst for me, so it actually took a long time to find out exactly who Nico really was. And for that matter - who anybody else was at the camp. Oblivious to all the big names and world champions I was hanging with, all I could think about were perfect pipes, and the tactics to make them work.

From the start it was phenomenal, all these past realisations coming true. For so long I had campaigned the rider/driver scene for park building and it took till Switzerland before I witnessed it first hand. There was no argument about product style, cat time, rosters or fear of responsibility. Just a driver and a team of pro-shapers, making what they want most, because that's what the customer wants and that is what the children deserve. Bang! Epic pipes for kids to learn on and champions to progress with. Tools for purposeful evolution.

Nico drove the cutter with the power of a man in love, again proving that this is a vital ingredient in anything we do. As we spent more time together it all began to unfold. Nicolas Vaudroz is a noble name in Swiss snowboarding from way back when. A true freerider. Heart and soul. Born and bred in Leysin - the heart of Europe - home to the most famous run of epic halfpipe events outside Vermont. Nicolas has been part of a lot.

Growing up mountain surfing with TonTon and heaps of great warriors, pushing the winter freedom movement and their balance from the roots up, smiles first. Nicolas you might say, has the mind to make things work through enjoyment. Giving riders like Terje and Ingemar quality riding during a time when it was still hard for riders to find perfect pipes. Before the days of transition cutters, when the only parks out there came from the heart and soul of unpaid riders. Lovers. So I listened and learned. Confirmed. All the things I had dreamt about - real functional pipes on a moving snow pack. It was so impressive. Nico was riding the pipe with us, shaping proud with a shovel in his hand. Tuning his transitions so that the next rider that dropped in would have the best opportunity to enjoy balance.

Then one day he said to me, " cat driving, or snowboarding for that matter, is only part of me. Seriously Pete, I am more of an artist." Then one night we all went to an exhibition he was having. It was so mind expanding. We spoke about the relationship between art and life, and the whole necessity to be creatively skilled in any endeavour. Of how education had been neglected in primitive lands and cherished in noble kingdoms. About the connection of all things and the power of love in thought.

The gift of light to us with active realisation and a common ambition for freedom. We got talking so far from boardriding and snow grooming that I started dreading the idea that the most amazing cat driver I have ever met, may some day stop pushing pipes.

After that I was hanging with Nico the artist not Nico the driver and the lessons just kept getting stronger. My eyes opening from the tunnel vision of boardriding just for bigger and better. Now, I was truly learning about snowboarding for oneself, for everybody. Inner balance so that all your chakras join to white and radiate brightness on everything in life. Feeling the story of the mountain, when you ride, words whispering of all-time. The story of our earth translated from the water cycle. Tales of oceans dancing across mountains through the rivers and the snow. Communication across the worlds. Listening to the universal spirit as it guides us from within.

During a special freeride session we talked stories of fairies and magic, of indigenous living and freedom, while exploring his backyard and hiking the Leysin Temple. Sven and Cyril by my side taking notes as well. Then we carved majestic turns together. Feeding off the wisdom that Nico had shared. A true noble and child of the Earth. Nicolas Vaudroz is one very peaceful and happy being. Stories of past lives as American Indians or an African Witch Doctor, don't seem strange. His smile is fully contagious and as time moves us, I begin to find the true heart behind the artist, behind the rider, behind the driver. Another messenger to help our world realise itself.

retrospective by pea ce

Pipe shapers from the heart

Transition warriors - Neri, McNally, Mermod

Terri Brunner

Cyril Neri

Cyril Neri & Nicole Angelrath

NOBLE CAUSE WARRIOR

When a rider flies higher
the feeling is epic!
Thanks to those
opening doors,
without them
there'd still
be wars.
Respect
to all
allowing
free choice
The Heartcore
helping kids play
The art, design and
story gifting inspiration.
Our most sincere appreciation.

Fredrik Sarvelle © Epic.

Homage to the noble cause warrior

Ninja heartcore jedi TonTon showing us da ho ho!

'TonTon Holland - Leysin heartcore © Epic.

144

Who is really in there? A question to be asked of oneself and answered through meditation. Traditional, artistic or athletic, meditation has a place in every calling, no success is without it. Sheridan knows it and so does Nico the humble Artist. - epic leysin

Random diary entry - It's the morning of another day in Swiss. Amazing place, strangely feels like home? Started my visit having a skate at Aigle train station waiting for Sven. Can finally ollie gutters, not every time but the streets are opening up. It always feels refreshing to skate. Bit sweaty for all the welcome hugs in Leysin. Chalet Valuga is ripe with energy.

Next day - I drove up the hill with Nicolas to groom the boardercross and pipe. It was a white out with heavy snow falling so we moved the maintenance schedule and got into a conversation about the swiss nobles. Which warmed my heart. Then rode down through fresh tracks so nice. Burning legs. Amazing to watch the great Vaudroz turn a snowboard. I wish I could be as he, so with every turn I try to roll out off my back foot and effortlessly pop airborne into the next turn. Yet it is harder than my friend makes it look. Like a ground hawk playing master to the quale, Nicolas danced and weaved around me as we re-kindled the sacred soul.

After, we went painting at Nico's little studio. Joyful first time art for me among amazing conversation with Sheridan and another friend. Such spiritual people, very warm, open and ready to laugh a lot.

Morning meditation at 6.45, exactly 20 minutes feels great. Still can't believe how perfect it works. Nico's ready so we go straight up to cut the pipe. Life is inspiring. Miss my girl. We groom park but not pipe. Then I ride the pipe for 3 hours - her kinked walls telling me I can do better, I'm telling her she can do better too. The boys comment some nice style and recommend I save my energy for the fresh cut tomorrow. Feeling like I need all the practice I can get I ride until my legs collapse, and then do one more run. Why go home angry from battle?

The snow turbo integra 7 pipe groomer, that has been developed partly through the Leysin heart, looks sensational. Nico speaks more stories of the Euro championship transitions built with shovels and brotherhood. I have similar stories about home too but our battle is still being won.

Chalet living is very uplifting. Long conversations on life love and the developing new world. The Swiss government (one of the most advanced and noble democracies I have felt) voted unanimously to organise the beneficial herb industry. Legalization? Now they'll take the vote to their people. Change against prejudice is so good for the human race. I am honoured to witness such shifts in consciousness during travel. There is an amazing connection with this Swiss heart, like they are blood. Much respect and thanks to Nico's hospitality and presence. He is such a great healer, as I no longer feel like a poor man.

Our family rejoice
in sharing smiles.
It's a beautiful life
if we choose it to be. Even
when things are down there
can still be some yippidy-dee!
Cheers to Leysin,
Nico, Cyril, Sven
& da SwissHeart.

Cyril in Leysin by Christophe Margot

Leysin Pyramid

Chalet Valluga

The Marmot

The call him 'Doc'

Nico backcountry by Christophe Margot

Meeting someone who knows freedom can give us many visions of possibility. Discoveries that our own walls are merely imaginations inside, developed from poor information or past misunderstandings. Ultimately confirming that what we choose to think creates our reality.

That said, it's possible that all our burdens have just been sold to us through misguidance -

meaning our keys to life are here already and have always been inside us. Simply live open and true to your beliefs and follow your own heart. Yes, we are all one, working together on this Earth. Yet the only truths lie within each individual. No-body else can really tell you what to do. Just be true to your word if you make an agreement and don't be afraid to say no if you feel so. The key to balance is a strength to fight for what is right in the light. The sunny day and laughter play.

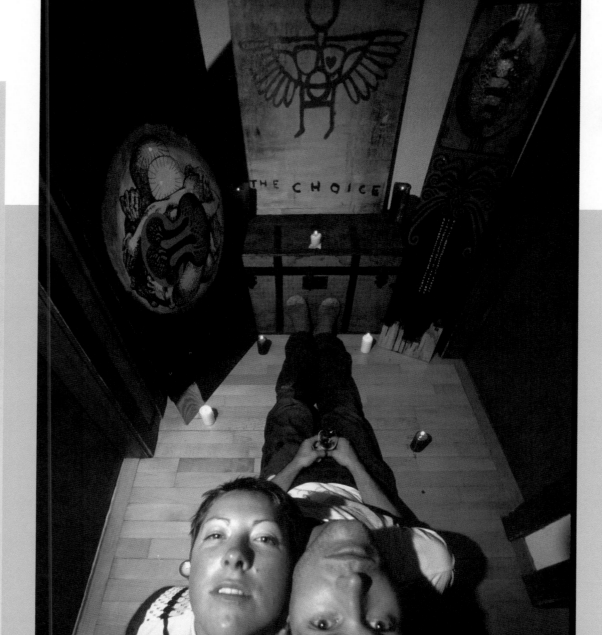

Wisdom for the people - Sherri & Nico - art for the mind - pea ce

This rock drop in Leysin *and the epic* Nendaz *powder photo oopposite* © Pat Vermeulen

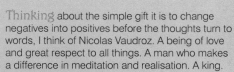
nicolas vaudroz

Thinking about the simple gift it is to change negatives into positives before the thoughts turn to words, I think of Nicolas Vaudroz. A being of love and great respect to all things. A man who makes a difference in meditation and realisation. A king.

Which brings us toward the end of this premier storybook. Thanks to all involved! I must say it's been pretty stressful, a few mistakes but none I can change. Will surely do things even better in the next epic story.

It's inspiration comes partly through Nico so I hope this premier has stoked you some and triggered a few feelings within about the great spirit. It's a re-readable, so soak it up any time you wish, or pass it on and spread the word. We are only in it to share the love.

Remember these are visions from our heart, uncovered by noble friends such as Nicolas and the Horseshoe crew. Plus all the global freedom core, you know who you are (pretty much every funky ass freerider anywhere from Whistler to Wyoming, Andora to Argentina, & Hotham to the Himalaya), everybody is making a difference. A positive difference. We can feel it, togetherness. Help the people of fear realise they can swap it for love. Show them how to ride, so they can see it's all in their minds. Practice balance, practice life. To score is to find epic times.

THIS
book is dedicated to the
family of Riddles. Sharing stories
about other worlds to unite us as one in
struggle, happiness then freedom. Forever thanks
to the Swiss heart, with love and respect to Jah,
our kangaroo spirit, and you, for being a part of what
already was and what always will be. Sharing stories
with wisdom through open communication. Special
appreciation to children, especially the ones who can
give without being asked. Also written in appreciation
to those who fight and sacrifice in the name of
balance, liberation and honour. Justice to
all! This the call of our
TIME.

Alex Coudray - Swiss Extreme Champion

So Alex
the verbier extreme
now you can tell all
there is merit in dreams
with roots music
herbal sensation
positive vibration
traveling the nations

Pea Ce © Justin Field

epic JOURNAL — Anticipation

epic JOURNAL

epic JOURNAL — Bigfella

epic JOURNAL — LEGENDS

epic JOURNAL — momentum

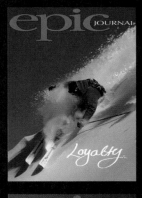

epic JOURNAL — Loyalty

epic JOURNAL — SESSIONS

epic JOURNAL — Pilgrimage

epic JOURNAL — Carnival

epic JOURNAL — winter heat

PETER CORNEY is a visionary, storyteller, freerider. Friends call him Pea Ce. For thirty years he chased snow seasons in Australia, USA, Japan, Canada, France, Switzerland and New Zealand. Working in diverse aspects of mountain culture. Founding member of the Summit Board Riders (SBR circa '91) it morphed into Summit Heartcore to campaign for everyone to find there own EpicBalance. After contributing to magazines and advertising as a model, photographer, writer and graphic designer, Pea Ce produced these works to expand his publishing and knowledge-sharing skills. Creating photo storylines to inspire one-love and equilibrium is Pete's passion @ **epicbalance.com**

SUMMIT HEART CORES

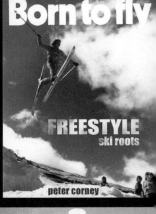

Born to fly

FREESTYLE ski roots

peter corney

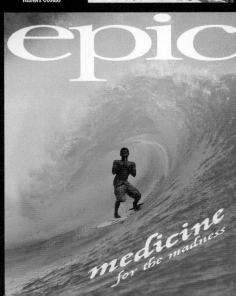

epic

medicine for the madness

Printed in Great Britain
by Amazon

85455897R00092